The Martial Application of the Rifle

By

Paul G. Markel

The Martial Application of
the Rifle

Paul G. Markel

Copr. 2022

All Rights Reserved

Cover Design: Zachary J. Markel

Dedication

This book is dedicated to the memory of my friend and firearms training mentor, James Yeager.

Yeager lived an unapologetic life and died an unapologetic death. Tens of thousands of men and women are better people thanks to his unwillingness to accept the status quo and not simply repeat training dogma.

Til Valhalla!

The Author (left) and James Yeager (right) on the range at Tactical Response in Camden, Tennessee.

Foreword

If you have read any of my previous books related to firearms, particularly the SOTG Instructor Development Manual, you will know that my first introduction to the rifle as a fighting tool came in the United States Marine Corps beginning in 1987. Prior to entering the Corps I had taken a 40 hour defensive pistol course from John S. Farnam so I knew my way around a handgun before enlisting.

Having spent my teenage years in rural Ohio, farm country, I would estimate that I personally created a few thousand empty .22 LR cases that decorated the landscape of Holmes and Wayne Counties. On my 18th birthday I drove directly from school to The Gun Shop in Wooster, Ohio and purchased a Ruger 10/22 .22 LR repeating rifle. Prior to that I borrowed .22 rifles from friends. My friends and I, aside from a few lectures on gun safety, were primarily self-taught. My grandfather had shown me how to line up the sights on a Daisy lever-action BB gun when I was 11 and I carried that experience to a .22 rifle.

Being teenage boys full of adventure, we were constantly looking for a challenge when it came to shooting our .22 rifles. Wandering through the fields we were on constant alert for groundhogs; a menace to farmers and cattle. A rural dump or landfill became a shooting gallery. I recall one time we found an old string of large (screw-in) Christmas lights. We took the dead light bulbs and placed them on top of wooden fence posts to test our accuracy.

My friends and I all purchased gun magazines. I was a big fan of Soldier of Fortune while in my teens. I would read articles written by combat veterans who extolled the virtues of the FN FAL, the German G3, and, of course, the AR-15 and the cool, compact version the CAR-15. I dreamed of someday being able to own an Uzi or a MAC-10.

When I enlisted in the Marine Corps in 1987, the standard service rifle at the time was the M-16A2. I learned that rifle inside and out and I qualified as an Expert at Parris Island. The primary focus of our initial training with the M-16A2 was precision marksmanship. For that I am most grateful because it gave me a solid background upon which to build my skills. It was not until I was assigned to 1st Battalion, 6th Marine Regiment in Camp Lejeune that I was able to work with the rifle as a close quarters fighting tool.

Our training with a fighting rifle at that time was good, but it was not what I would call *great.* You see, after Vietnam, the US Military fell into a Cold War mentality. All of the focus for the Pentagon was big ticket items: ICBMs, Aircraft Carriers, Nuclear Submarines, and long distance bombers. When it came to training and gear for the average infantryman, those came a far second behind the big stuff. Our annual allotment for training ammunition was measured in hundreds of rounds per man, per year. The Pentagon would spend billions of dollars on missiles and bombers but held the purse string tight for small arms ammunition for training.

When I left active-duty the first time, I became a police officer and fired thousands of rounds through my service pistols and somewhat fewer through our patrol shotguns. For rifle training I was on my own.

The absolute best, most forward thinking private training with a combat rifle that I took after departing from the Corps was the Fighting Rifle course at Tactical Response in Camden,

Tennessee. I took that course not quite twenty years ago as these words are typed. James Yeager and his instructor corps took a hard look at modern rifle training and questioned almost everything that was being taught. James kept what he saw as valuable and discarded the rest that was out of date.

Ironically, after 9/11/01 and our subsequent involvement in the failed Global War on Terror, the training that they average infantryman had with a rifle was woefully out of date. The US Military spent the first few years of GWOT catching up with the realities of the modern battlefield and non-linear combat tactics.

As a Military Contractor, I was a part of a training team that taught Small Arms & Tactics to troops prior to deployment to combat zones. One of the biggest issues of which we had to deal with was getting past the "cold range" out of date training techniques that were left over from an era when we did not actually have troops engaged in combat.

For several years, I was able to train thousands of troops to use the M4 and also the M9 Beretta as close quarters fighting tools. Getting career military Officers and NCOs to let go of outdated Cold War training concepts was not an easy task. Nonetheless, I come to the pages of this book with decades of experience both employing and teaching people how to employ a self-loading rifle in a combat fashion. It is my sincere hope to be able to pass on what I have learned over the last three decades or so to you and for you to find value in this information.

Paul G. Markel
Wyoming, June 2022

BRN-177E2 5.56mm

Please go to www.SOTGU.com for more information about Rifle employment and other training courses.

Contents

Introduction

The primary function of this introduction is to establish the main purpose of this text and to clarify our mission. Firearms can be enjoyed by many people and used for myriad purposes. If you are an American citizen, the right to possess arms is a birthright that no politician has the authority to deny you, although many will never stop trying.

If you live in any country besides the United States of America, firearms ownership is a regulated privilege and an expensive one at that. For socialist / authoritarian nations, charging large fees for the privilege to own a gun is par for the course. In our world prior to the United States, it was always the wealthy elitists, and of course the governments who stole the people's money via taxes, who could afford to possess arms.

Throughout the history of firearms, they have been used in hunting, in competitions or games, collected as objects of affection, used by governments to defeat their enemies and oppress their citizens, and lastly in the interest of self-defense and to stand against tyranny.

At Student of the Gun, we have asserted from the beginning that a firearm, a gun, must always be considered an *Instrument of Liberty* by free men, citizens not slaves. The moment you begin to view a gun as a tool used for recreation, for hunting, for engaging in games and sport, you lose the understanding as to why the Citizens of the United States were assured the unalienable right to possess arms.

American citizens have many unalienable rights, but they do not have a "right" to hunt (hunting is not once mentioned in the US Constitution), to play games, or to collect objects for recreation. The right to keep and bear arms comes from the unalienable right to protect *LIFE and LIBERTY.*

Regarding rifles, there are certainly many enjoyable recreational activities that you can engage in and that is all well and good. The reason that I choose to title this book "The Martial Application of the Rifle" is to make clear that our focus herein is not sports or recreation, but the use of a rifle as a tool to defend both Life and Liberty from those who would seek to take either or both.

It is true that certain principles and fundamentals crossover between fighting with a rifle or shooting a match or even taking game in hunting. Fundamental marksmanship applies to all because the gun is inanimate, it does not know nor care for which purpose it is being used. However, there will be times when the application and tactical employment that we recommend will vary from what might be common in recreation or games. With that being said, please continue.

"This is the law. The purpose of fighting is to win. There is no possible victory in defense. The sword is more important than the shield, and skill is more important than either. The final weapon is the brain. All else is supplementary."
John Steinbeck

*Author's Note: As always, it is recommended that prior to reading this book that you grab a pencil for notetaking and a highlighter of some sort.

Chapter 1 Understanding Power Tools

During a previous text, the Precision Rifle Range Book, I went into great detail regarding the fundamentals of rifle marksmanship. During this text, I will refer to many of those as they apply to the subject of using a self-loading rifle in a martial or combat fashion.

Thanks to the engineering genius of men like Gene Stoner, Mikhail Kalashnikov, Dieudonné Saive we in our modern era have access to some of the most efficient and effective tools ever to be possessed by free men to be used as instruments of liberty.

For the laymen in the audience; Stoner invented the AR-10 and the AR-15, Kalashnikov invented the AK-47/AKM, and Saive invented the FN FAL. Yes, there were other engineers on the teams of the aforementioned men, save your letters. Also, we should acknowledge that many of these men stood on the shoulders of men such as John Browning and John Garand. I would also be remiss if I did not acknowledge the influence of Hugo Schmeisser, the engineer who created the Stg-44 Sturmgewehr.

During our discussion of the martial application of the rifle, we will be considering the self-loading, repeating rifle or carbine that is fed via some type of detachable magazine. The modern AR, AKM, FAL, and many others will fall into this category.

According to a survey by the communist-run American media, the number of Stoner-based AR-15 style rifles in circulation in the United States of America exceeds 20 million. The tally for the AKM style, the Mini-14, and myriad others is essentially unknown. However, it is safe to say that since 2005, the American Rifle (AR) has become the #1, top selling self-loading centerfire rifle in the USA. (Save your letters, I know the original AR stood for *Armalite Rifle)*

While a self-loading, magazine fed repeater, like the AR and AK can be used as a distance weapon for precision tasks, the primary function of these firearms is to be used as a power tool. During the previous book where we addressed the Martial Application of the Shotgun, we used that term.

In a self-defense scenario, the faster you can stop a threat, with the fewest number of rounds fired, the better off the good people are. We carry handguns because they are small, light, and convenient. We do not carry handguns because they are the best fight stoppers. When it comes to stopping a human predator from killing you, from a ballistic standpoint, a handgun is a relatively poor choice compared to the 12 gauge shotgun or the centerfire rifle.

I'll give you a perfect real world example. During the 1980's and 1990's American law enforcement tactical teams fell in love with the HK MP5 chambered in 9x19mm. The use of a CAR-15 in 5.56mm seemed to be *overkill* or *too much gun.* However, what police agencies discovered was that when using the 9mm, deadly threats required numerous hits to stop and, very often, the relatively slow and heavy 9mm bullets passed through and put innocent bystanders at risk.

After 9/11/01 and moving into the GWOT era, police tactical units slowly began to switch over to AR style guns chambered in 5.56mm. What they discovered during real world deadly force encounters was the human attackers stopped faster, requiring fewer shots to be fired, and the pass through rate for the 5.56mm rifle round was LESS than that from the MP5 in 9x19mm. Yes, Virginia, there is a Santa Claus and the 5.56mm/.223 Remington proved to be a better overall choice than the 9mm fired from a subgun.

Despite what your great Uncle Joe has said about the .223 Remington being a "gopher round" unfit to stop deadly attackers, 20 full years of combat has proven that bad guys do indeed stop and die when shot with it, particularly during close quarters combat. The advances in that cartridge since Vietnam have made it a truly effective urban combat load. The Mk262 round uses a 77 grain OTM (open-tip match) bullet which is also referred to as the BTHP or boat-tail hollow point. I personally dropped a 250 pound feral hog at a distance of 25 yards with a single shot of the Mk262 from Black Hills Ammunition. For those unfamiliar with the taking of feral hogs in the United States, they are tough, strong, resilient animals with thick hides. In this specific case, it was nighttime and the hog was coming at us in knee high Texas prairie grass. The pucker factor was intense.

I have a friend who shot an insurgent in Iraq with a single Mk262 round from a precision tuned AR. As was standard operating procedure, the insurgent was taken to an Army field hospital. The surgeon who worked on the terrorist, he expired, thought that the man had been shot with a 7.62mm sniper rifle. My friend had to tell the doctor that he actually shot him with a 5.56mm.

My point in relating all of the above is this, while many Americans believe that pistols are for close-in work and rifles are saved for distance work, when your life is threatened by a deadly attacker it be better to rely upon ballistic and historical facts. The fact is, an AR loaded in modern .223 Remington/5.56mm is a far better home defense gun than any handgun could ever hope to be.

Before we continue let's put to bed some of the confusion about .223 Remington versus the 5.56x45mm NATO round. Rather than give my personal opinion, I will go directly to those who make ammunition for a living. Here is a direct quote from the Hornady Ammunition Law Enforcement website:

*The first difference is the **higher pressure level of the 5.56 NATO cartridge** which runs at approximately 58,000 psi. A .223 Remington is loaded to approximately 55,000 psi. The second and most important difference between the two is the fact that a 5.56 NATO chamber has a .125" longer throat.*

Think of the .223 versus 5.56 as .38 Special +P compared to .357 Magnum. Rifles chambered in a true 5.56mm NATO will chamber and fire the .223 Remington cartridge. A rifle chambered specifically for .223 Remington should NOT be loaded with 5.56mm NATO. The invention of the .223 Wylde chamber has given us a best of both world option, at least in the opinion of some. Rifles chambered in .223 Wylde will feed, cycle, and shoot both of the previous loads equally well. It is for this reason that many firearms manufacturers are offering guns with .223 Wylde chambers. For example, the BRN-180 rifles built by Brownells have a Wylde chamber. Acknowledgement and appreciation to Mr. Bill Wylde for this design.

Another reason the self-loading rifle is a better choice for home defense versus a handgun is simply physics. With a rifle you have 4 points of contact to control the gun; two hands, shoulder mount and stock weld. With a handgun you have one or two points of contact; a single or both hands. Also, the sight radius for a rifle is longer thus reducing the margin of error when aiming the firearm versus a pistol. These facts are not complicated and the physical realities are not altered by human perception or feelings to the contrary.

Nearly two decades ago I was training at Gunsite Academy. The question was put to us like this; "In five seconds, three cracked out assholes are going to break down your front door. On the table is an AR-15 with 10 rounds and a GLOCK 17 with 10 rounds. You have only 5 seconds to choose one of them. Which one will you choose?"

Again, if you answer that question minus personal feelings or opinions, the answer is simple and straightforward. You would be foolish to leave the AR on the table and pick up the GLOCK (nothing against GLOCK here). Now, having all the time in the world to prepare yourself for a deadly home invasion, to include going to training to learn how to use the tools effectively, what would you decide to choose?

Yes, people get all tripped up talking about opening doors and turning on light switches, etc. In the end, we must be honest and address the purpose of self-defense. The purpose of self-defense is to stop the deadly threat as quickly and effectively as humanly possible. Preconceived notions about pistols and rifles are irrelevant.

Gun shop rumors and internet forum bullshit are not something we should be using to make potential life and death decisions. We choose to use a self-loading rifle as a personal defense tool not because it is a long distance, precision weapon, we arm ourselves with a rifle because it is a power tool.

Chapter 2 Choosing the Correct Tool

Once more, before you get your back hairs up and tell me you don't like the AR because great Uncle Joe convinced you that it is a gopher gun, I don't care what you choose. You are an American, buy what you want to.

If you don't like the Stoner design, fine. I don't have stock in Stoner. The Kalashnikov will fill the bill just as well. Don't like that? Fine, the SIG MCX uses what is basically a modern version of Stoner's AR-180 or Armalite rifle bolt/action design. HK and the many HK clones have roller-lock actions that chamber both the 5.56mm and 7.62 NATO. The Garand action can be found on the Ruger Mini-14 and the M1 Carbine self-loading guns. Don't like any of these? Buy the SA58, a faithful replica of the FN FAL from DS Arms.

Occam Defense ODS-1775 7.62x39mm

If you want to emulate the Europeans; Steyr and IWI both make bullpup action, self-loading rifles. These are particularly attractive choices for people to have a lot of disposable income to spend on guns. Recently, Springfield Armory jumped into the bullpup market with the Hellion, a $2000 American made version of the bullpup. Kel-Tec has the RDB which is a bit more economical.

IWI Tavor 5.56mm

Speaking of economy, how much should you be willing to spend on your self-loading, magazine fed rifle? In this day and age that is a tremendously loaded question as the price of guns goes up and down like a proverbial rollercoaster.

Suffice it to say that when it comes time to choose a tool with which you will potentially save your life and the lives of your family, bargain shopping is probably not the way to go. If all remains constant as I write this, expect to pay $750 to $1000 for a well made rifle from a reliable manufacturer.

Now we come to the question, who is a "reliable manufacturer"? Good question. Let's consider companies who have made their living producing firearms for decades or even centuries. Okay, here goes; Colt (now owned by CZ and that is a good thing), BCM (Bravo Company Manufacturing), Daniel Defense, Stag Arms, Armalite, LMT, LWRC, SIG, and FN. If you want the best AK made in the USA, contact Occam Defense. Yes, there are many more, but the aforementioned have a good track record for quality and reliability, as well as government contracts.

Are there smaller manufacturers that make good guns? Sure. However, we are in a buyer beware situation. Last year a man showed up for a rifle class with a $2500 custom AR and the gun was basically a single-shot. The poor guy had to constantly clear stoppages. When he contacted the maker, they explained to him that it needed a 200 round break-in period. Folks, in our modern era, I'm going to call bullshit on that. Yes, the break-in period can be a real thing, but for self-loading, magazine fed Stoner-based rifle, the idea that you need to spend $100 plus on ammo in order for the gun to function is more than I would be willing to accept.

DS Arms SA-58 (FAL) 7.62x51mm NATO

I'm not sure when the term "battle rifles" became vogue, but in our modern vernacular, people have started referring to self-loading, magazine fed rifles that chamber the 7.62mm NATO cartridge as such. This is where the AR-10 and its many variations now fall.

From my personal experience of testing firearms over 30 years, I have found that there is a very good reason why the AR-10 came first and the AR-15 in 5.56mm came second. The 5.56mm version runs better and is more reliable. As cool as the AR-10 or the .308 Winchester AR might seem, finding one that will function with the same reliability as the smaller versions can be quite a difficult task. Yes, again there are some .308 ARs that do run. However, the truth is that just as many of them are extremely finicky eaters and they can be as moody as a menstruating woman.

Before you tell me that your AR-10 runs "flawlessly" tell me whether or not you have taken a two day class and put 300-400 rounds through the gun. Firing twenty rounds from the shooting bench is not exactly a true reliability test. Also, expect to pay about $300 to $500 more for an AR-10 compared to the same make of AR-15.

The HK G3 in 7.62 NATO has a bit of a cult following and my experience is that as long as you keep them clean and well-lubed, they will run reliably. These roller-lock guns do however require dedicated maintenance. If you are an AK, "clean it once a year" guy, the G3 is not for you.

Many Americans are in love with the civilian version the M14 from Springfield Armory simply known as the M1A. I have experience with both the military M14 and the M1A. Springfield makes a short "SOCOM" version of the M1A and in my humble opinion, these rifles should be shipped with a complementary mouthguard. The SOCOM will shake your fillings loose.

The FN FAL is a Cold War era battle rifle that was produced under license by at least a dozen countries during the height of its popularity. Although FN discontinued new production of the FAL many years ago, there are still good guns to be found. DS Arms is the US manufacturer of the SA58, a faithful reproduction of the original guns.

Due to the fact that the 5.56mm NATO has been so popular for the last 40 years or so, people will again fall back on the thought process that the 7.62x51mm NATO cartridge is best used for long distance precision, not close quarters combat. While it is true that for several decades the US Military sniper rifles have been built around that cartridge, a gun such as the FAL is also suited for close combat.

During the Rhodesian Bush War, which lasted 15 years, the Rhodesian Light Infantry engaged communist terrorists in the bush at close quarters. These soldiers trained to rapidly mount the rifles and double-tap "terrs" (African slang for terrorists) at ranges of only fifteen, twenty or twenty-five meters. No, the recoil from the 7.62mm was not too several for rapid doubles. That is actually one of the amazing things about the FAL. That rifle was built and designed so well that rapid target engagement was a reality for well-trained troops. Talk about a sledgehammer!

Once more, you are an American and can buy whatever you like. If you must have a .308 Winchester/7.62 NATO self-loading rifle, I would take a long hard look at the SA58 from DS Arms.

Chapter 3 Training: Running the Machine

In regard to training with a self-loading, magazine-fed rifle, there are numerous similarities when it comes to running the machine. The mount and grip and trigger press and sight alignment for most all rifles remains constant. Naturally, there are also many gun specific idiosyncrasies that will apply only to a particular make or model. Herein lies my conundrum, do I try to lump all fighting rifles together or do I address each one as an individual entity?

Naturally, this is the same issue that Small Arms and Tactics instructors must face when they have a class full of students who have brought a variety of makes and models of rifle along with them. Instructors that teach units or agencies have it easy in this regard because all of their students are issued the exact same guns and gear. I have had to deal with both situations.

I suppose that it is best to split the difference here. First I will address gun handling techniques that apply regardless of the tool at hand. Unique model specifics will be addressed as this chapter continues.

Consistent Gun Handling

The key to mastery with any tool, particularly a firearm, is to handle or operate the gun in a consistently correct fashion. For our discussion of the martial application of the rifle, we will handle our firearms as though they are tools to be used in combat, not toys to be used for games.

Dominant and Support Hands

By this stage in the game you should know which hand is your dominant hand and which one is your support hand. Your dominant hand should correspond with your dominant eye, it does not matter for our purposes if this is right or left.

When we are handling a fighting tool, the dominant hand holds the grip area of the weapon. Most of the rifles we will be using will have a pistol grip. In the case of the M1 Carbine or the Mini-14 with standard wooden stocks, you will hold the angled grip area. If you are in the People's Republik of Kalifornia and have some weird paddle/flipper /doohickey hanging off of your gun, there is nothing I can do for you.

Now that we have determined that the dominant hand holds onto and controls the rifle, we should understand that the support hand performs all of the other duties. These duties will include locating a magazine and inserting it into the gun. The support hand also operates the charging handle. During stoppage clearing, the support hand is tasked with the basic fixing of the gun. Of course, during shooting the support hand is the one that holds onto the forend or forward portion of the rifle.

What we are attempting to eliminate is the amateurish behavior of constantly swapping hands back and forth on the rifle. This is a waste of time, hampers consistency and creates muscle confusion under the high stress of a lethal force encounter.

Most, but not all, rifles are built in a way that allows the dominant hand to disengage the manual safety. Also, the majority of rifles are built assuming that the shooter will be right handed. Sorry, sinister folks. Fear not, with a bit of training, lefties can learn to operate a standard right-handed rifle without much problem. Even left handed people can operate a standard AR-15 minus ambi controls.

*Author's Note: For thirty plus years I have witnessed the desire of aftermarket accessory makers to create ambidextrous safety levers, charging handles, bolt-hold open devices, etc. The vast majority of these devices detract from the reliability of the gun, this is particularly true with ambi safety levers on AR rifles. Before you spend hundreds of dollars trying to modify your rifle, take the stock rifle to a training course and learn how to use it as is.

Also, it should be the aim and focus of every shooter with martial aspirations to be able to run whichever gun they have in hand. For instance, if you are a lefty and have all of your personal guns tricked out with special ambi controls, what are you going to do if you don't have your *special gun* and someone hands you a stock AR or a stock AK? Will you be able to run that machine?

Points of Contact

As mentioned earlier on, one of the reasons why a long gun is inherently more accurate or less sensitive to aiming errors is due to the fact that you have four points of contact on a rifle. The stock should be placed in the shoulder pocket on the dominant side consistently. Also, the stockweld or cheek weld, where the shooter's cheek bone touches the stock must be repeated consistently as well. Our dominant hand grips and controls the gun the same way and we place our support hand in the same place each time.

When the shooter learns to make every single point of contact with the rifle consistent, their natural point of aim will be developed and the muzzle will be directed toward the target rapidly and reliably. With this accomplished, all that is required now is for the shooter to use their dominant eye to fine tune the sight picture / target picture. At close quarters distances, consistent, repeatable gun mount will cause the muzzle to be indexed on the threat. This allows the shooter to put extremely rapid shots on target. Minus consistency in regard to the points of contact, that becomes more and more difficult.

One of the many drills that we required our military shooters to perform was to engage targets during lowlight/darkness. When using the M4, the first drill was fired from only 15 meters. No flashlights were used, only ambient light from strategically staged vehicles illuminated the silhouettes. Our shooters used standard M4 iron sights, no red dots. Those who fared the best were the shooters with consistent gun mount and a naturally developed point of aim.

We did the same drill with the M9 service pistols from five meters. Again, even though they could not make out their sights in the darkness, a consistent, natural point of aim allowed them to get reliable hits on target.

Four Points of Contact

Loading the Machine

When it comes to loading the rifle, the shooter will hold and control the gun with their dominant hand with the muzzle up and the magazine well rotated in the direction of the support hand. The shooter's eyes are up, looking down range toward threats, not at the gun.

The support hand locates a magazine, grips in around the center for maximum control. Ken Hackathorn calls this the "beer can" hold. For the AR or similar rifles, the magazine is inserted straight up into the magazine well until it stops. An audible 'click' might be heard or it might not. Before releasing the magazine, the shooter gives it a slight tug to ensure it is locked in place. Notice that I did not say *tap* the magazine. If you load as I just described, there is no need to tap. "So what if I tap?" you just said, "it's not hurting anything." What I have witnessed is that the loading tap becomes two taps, then three and the process morphs into a nervous tick.

Next, the support hand immediately locates the charging handle and draws it vigorously to the rear placing maximum compression on the recoil spring. The support hand releases the charging handle allowing the spring compression to do its job and chamber a round. With the action completed, the support hand moves to the forend to hold the rifle and the shooter now has a loaded firearm. That's it.

It is imperative that the running of the charging handle becomes an instinctive process after the magazine is inserted. We do not carry half-loaded rifles for fighting. If you are afraid to carry a rifle with a loaded chamber you need more confidence and training. If you desire for the rifle to be unloaded, do not put a magazine in it.

Loading Again

After the initial loading process, if the shooter engages targets and fires the rifle, it needs to be loaded again if additional magazines are available. To *Load Again,* we repeat the loading process exactly as described during the previous section. This is done regardless of the bolt being rearward on an empty magazine or forward on a partially loaded magazine.

Keep in mind that many rifles, particularly the AK variants, do NOT lock open on an empty magazine. There may also be times that even the AR bolt for one reason or another does not lock open on empty. By training properly, we address this situation. We do not rely on the bolt being opened or closed to determine how we run the machine.

Addressing the Target

As with the shotgun in the previous text, a long gun is held or carried either muzzle down (muzzle pointed 12 inches from center of the legs) or muzzle up (at the sky, above head level). There are valid reasons for both types of carry and both must be practiced and trained.

Muzzle Down: with a loaded rifle in hand, the rifle is held securely by both hands, for right handers, the rifle is rolled so the ejection port is facing away from the body and stock is resting on the upper chest. For left handers, the ejection port is toward the body.

To address the target, the rifle is rolled up so the butt of the stock is in the shoulder pocket. As the rifle comes up, the dominant hand deactivates the manual safety. The shooter indexes the muzzle on target and is ready to fire.

Addressing the Target

Muzzle Up: again, with a loaded rifle, the support hand pushes the rifle out, pointing the muzzle at the target and then immediately pulls the butt into the shoulder pocket. As this is happening, the dominant hand will disengage the manual safety.

The 'thrust and pull' action is done to ensure that the stock is placed in the shoulder pocket in a consistently correct fashion. This also keeps the stock from catching or dragging against clothing or load-bearing gear during the mounting process.

Transitioning

If the shooter is carrying a sidearm in addition to their long gun, the primary answer to a stoppage with the rifle is to sling the gun and retrieve a working handgun to continue the fight. When fighting is no longer necessary or sufficient cover fire is being given, fix the stoppage.

In order to accomplish this task in a rapid fashion, the sling must already be over the shooter's neck/shoulders. This can be done using either a single point or a traditional two-point sling.

If the shooter has no secondary weapons, they must fix the stoppage to their long gun in a manner prescribed below. Transitioning from a long gun to a handgun is a skill that must be practiced in order for it to become natural and instinctive during a genuine fight for your life.

Stoppages

Because our repeating rifle functions in a similar fashion to the semi-automatic handgun, the stoppage types and clearing procedures will be consistent with what we should have already learned.

TYPE 1 Failure to Fire

A Type 1 stoppage is the quintessential 'Click, No Boom'. You press the trigger and instead of firing, it goes 'click'. This occurs 99 times out of 100 due to the shooter failing to chamber a round. You may also have a 'No Click, No Boom' situation where for whatever reason, the hammer is forward and the trigger has been disengaged.

Step 1: Support hand taps the base of the magazine firmly, ONE time.

Step 2: The support hand runs the charging handle vigorously in an identical fashion to the loading process.

Step 3: Attempt to fire if necessary.

TYPE 2 Stove Pipe

The Type 2 stoppage occurs during the firing cycle when an object, primarily a piece of spent brass, is impeding the bolt from closing and locking. The clearing process is identical to the Type 1. *Angle the ejection port to the ground.

Type 2 Stove Pipe

TYPE 3 Double-Feed

A Type 3 stoppage is also referred to as a 'double-feed'. Two objects are attempting to enter the chamber and the gun will not fire or cycle. Typically, a Type 3 is discovered after a rapid Type 1 fix has been attempted.

Step 1: Seek Cover, if no cover is available, drop to a knee and get low.

Step 2: Lock the bolt / action to the rear to relieve recoil spring pressure.

Step 3: Remove the ammunition source, if only one magazine is available, secure it under the dominant arm against the body.

Step 4: Using the support hand, vigorously work the action back and forth, once, twice, three times with the ejection port angled toward the ground.

Step 5: Use the support hand to insert a fresh magazine. If the only magazine is under the dominant arm, retrieve it and insert it as you would during the loading procedure.

Step 6: Use the support hand to run the bolt as you would for the loading procedure.

Step 7: Attempt to fire if necessary.

Type 3 Double Feed

TYPE 4 Bolt Override

Many readers might be shocked to encounter a Type 4 stoppage. This stoppage, though rare, can be particularly maddening as it is what we also refer to as a bolt override. This is primarily an issue with the AR series; a piece of brass or ammunition has become trapped above the bolt carrier group. The carrier key / gas key is keeping it in place and the bolt will not move.

Step 1: Seek Cover or drop to a knee to reduce your profile.

Step 2: Remove the ammunition source.

Step 3: Drop to a kneeling position if you have not already.

Step 4: Remove the magazine.

Step 5: Grip the weapons firmly using both the support and dominant hands. The dominant hand will grab the stock of the rifle.

Step 6: Slam the butt of the stock onto the ground vigorously until the bolt moves. In the military this is often called the "mortar" technique.

Step 7: With the obstruction cleared from the bolt, load the rifle as you would normally.

Step 8: Attempt to fire if necessary.

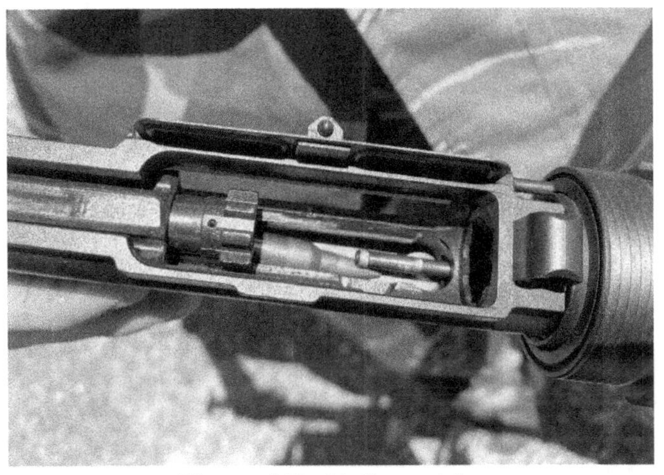

Type 4 Bolt Override

*Author's Note: All of the previous will work with most magazine fed rifles. The AK does not have a bolt hold open feature on standard models, therefore for a Type 3, the dominant hand will have to pull open the action while the support hand removes the magazine for clearing.

The author in the field with troops as a Small Arms & Tactics Instructor.

Chapter 4 Martial Application of the Rifle

One of the biggest misconceptions that people will have or excuses that they will put forward is that marksmanship fundamentals are important for distance shooting, but not for close quarters fighting with a rifle. Whether you are engaging a threat at 5, 25, 50, or 100 yards you are always responsible for the shots you take.

Just because we are shooting multiple rounds at relatively close distances does not mean we should take the fundamentals of marksmanship for granted. Trained shooters do not spray and pray, they put every shot where it needs to be.

The primary difference between employing a rifle in a slow-fire, precision fashion and the martial application of the rifle is that the latter situation tends to be far more dynamic. For the martial application of the rifle, we expect that the shooter will be moving; forward or back, left or right. We also expect them to be firing from awkward shooting positions, particularly from behind cover.

In order to employ a rifle in a dynamic fashion and still maintain accuracy, we will adhere to certain marksmanship fundamentals.

Rifle Mount

As we mentioned previously, consistency is the key to success when using firearms. When we mount the rifle in our shoulder pocket we do so in a consistent way. We place our cheek against the stock in the same place for every shot. Both our dominant and support hand hold the rifle firmly in the same position. Our elbows are relaxed and tucked down close to our rib cage, not sticking out like chicken wings.

Trigger Press

We place the finger print area or pad of our trigger finger directly on the center portion of the trigger. When we press the trigger we do so as if we are pressing it straight back toward our body. Trigger press is another form of consistency that we maintain. We learn our weapon and we learn the feel of the trigger. We train and practice so as to master the pressing of the trigger. We eliminate jerking or mashing the trigger in some spasmodic way.

Elbows down, no chicken wings.

Sight Alignment / Sight Picture

Whether using iron sights or an optic of some sort, our sight alignment and sight picture must be consistent. Sight alignment involves the shooter's dominant eye, the rear sight and the front sight. Sight picture is the relationship of the sights on the target.

Most AR's with iron sights have a rear peep and a front post. While we are on the subject of AR rear sights, if you have the traditional A2 rear sight with the flip up/fold back design, the aperture will have small and large hole options. For our purposes, we will put the large hole up and use it.

The majority of stock AK's have a rear notch and a front post. The elevation slide on the AK rear sight should be all the way back to the "100" setting.

Regardless of the rear sight set up, our dominant eye looks through the rear to find the front. The front sight post or blade is placed high in the upper chest area of a humanoid target or at the largest visible portion of the target if it is obstructed.

Naturally, the advantage of a 1:1 electronic optic with a red or green reticle is simplicity and ease of use. The sight alignment portion is merely finding the illuminated reticle and then placing it on the target for a sight picture. An optic allows for more rapid sight acquisition and placement on target. Also, along with a mastered trigger press, an optic allows very rapid initial and follow up shot placement.

However, keep in mind, it does not matter how expensive or Gucci your optic might happen to be, the scope does not shoot the rifle. We use quality gear to enhance our skill not to make up for a lack of it.

Addressing the Threat

Whether you begin from muzzle down or muzzle up, when you present the rifle to the target your shoulders should be squared up and slightly forward of your hips, pressing into the stock. Your feet will likely begin about shoulder width apart, but that does not have to be the case. Our toes will be pointed toward the target, not blades or angled off in odd directions.

A moving target is more difficult to hit, therefore we will refrain from taking multiple shots from a stationary position unless we are shooting from behind cover. With that being said, our goal for a "shooting stance" is simply to maintain our balance and not fall over. The exact position of your feet is basically irrelevant unless they are pointed outward like a clown. Remember, we are discussing dynamic movement with the rifle, not stationary slow-fire.

When addressing a threat in a rapid fashion with our self-loading rifle, we will fire two or three rapid shots onto it. Your ability to deliver the double or triple tap will depend on your level of skill and the relationship of the target both in distance and movement.

Humanoid targets inside of ten yards can easily be engaged with a double or triple tap by a trained shooter. The farther the distance to the target and the target's movement or lack thereof will determine how rapidly you can place well-aimed shots on it.

"How fast should I shoot?" is a question many might be asking. The answer is that you should be shooting only as fast or rapidly as you can make hits. The more training you have and practice you undergo, the better equipped you will be to make that decision.

For those who might say that a double or triple tap is possible with the light 5.56/.223, but not possible with "heavy calibers" like the 7.62x39mm or 7.62 NATO, I will remind you that the Rhodesians were double tapping "terrs" with the FAL in 7.62x51mm NATO.

Again, how rapidly you address the threat will depend on your level of skill with the equipment you have in your hands. Illuminated dot optics in a 1:1 configuration aid the shooter in rapid target engagement. We have twenty years of combat experience to back up that statement. That does not mean that skilled shooters cannot rapidly address targets with iron sights. This comes down to the training level and dedication of the individual to improve their skills.

F.A.S.T.

As mentioned in previous texts, the old method for training to engage dangerous humans was to fire, lower the gun slightly to look over it, and then to glance left and right over our shoulders. That was fine for the time, but we could do better.

James Yeager and Tactical Response adopted the acronym F.A.S.T. to help shooters remember how to train and practice so they would do the right thing during the heat of combat.

F - Fight: Address the threat and shoot it with as many rounds as needed to make it stop trying to kill you.

A - Assess: Look at what you did or check your work. Is the target actually down or did you merely wound the target and he/she is trying to get to cover so they can shoot you?

S - Scan: This is when we go MUZZLE UP and conduct a 360° scan of the world around us. As mentioned in previous books, we would call this the "check your world" portion. You are looking for both good guys and bad guys.

T - Top Off: Now is the time to put a fresh, fully loaded magazine in your rifle. This would be the *Load Again* method that we addressed previously. *Note: we always run the bolt / action when we load again. Which is better to have, an empty chamber and a magazine with 28 rounds, or a loaded chamber and 27 rounds?

The simple rule that we apply to martial shooting is, if we make noise with the gun, before we put it away, sling it, whatever, we load it again. If we did not make any noise with the previously loaded gun, we leave it alone.

Chapter 5 Mindset and Tactics

Tactics is when the shooter employs the gray matter between their ears and puts thoughts and practices to work in the real world. The hierarchy of combat with arms is; Mindset, Tactics, Skill, and Gear.

Your mindset determines every choice you make. Mindset determines whether or not you actually spend the time and money to attend professional training. Mindset determines whether or not your gun is ready to go when you need it. And, as you might have already guessed, mindset determines how you apply tactics in a mortal combat or martial environment.

Cover and Concealment

Concealment is any material that prevents the enemy from seeing you. Concealment can be a brick wall, a bunch of bushes, or a well-placed smoke grenade or two. In a way, even a good camouflage uniform can be a form of concealment.

Cover is any material that is likely to stop incoming small arms fire. Cover can also be concealment, but concealment alone is not cover.

One of the best tactical pieces of advice I received came during my very first professional firearms training courses. John Farnam said to us, "You must always be cover conscious." What he meant was that we should always be aware of our surroundings to the point where we could immediately and instinctively move toward cover.

For decades, James Yeager has been posing a question to his students, "What is more important in a gunfight, shooting the bad guy or not getting shot?" The question is not rhetorical. When analytical thought is applied, the answer is "Not getting shot." This is where cover consciousness comes into play.

Also, we must remember that *All Cover is Temporary*, this another tactical concept that we must acknowledge. By *temporary* we mean that if a bad guy knows you are behind a piece of cover they will either hammer it with everything they have in an effort to destroy it or they will move to circumvent your cover.

One of the phrases I use when discussing cover with my students is, "You cannot live behind cover." Cover gives us the opportunity to be protected from incoming fire while we quickly formulate a tactical plan. We have all seen movies where the heroes get down behind cover and have witty conversations while the bad guy stands in the same place dumping magazine after magazine at them with no effect. In the real world, the bad guy will simply move to get a better angle on you and kill you.

When caught in the open, minus immediate cover, your best cover will be a wall of lead directed at your attacker while you move your feet in an effort to get to cover. If there is simply no cover to be had, we drop down to our knees or to the prone position in order to make ourselves a more difficult target and return fire.

Another aspect to consider with cover is to keep some distance from it. If you hug or press against cover this action limits your peripheral vision and situational awareness as well as your ability to move away from it quickly.

Also, cover is generally also concealment. If you are using cover to prevent the threat from seeing you, you do not want to give away your exact position by resting your rifle on top of or on the side of cover. Shooting over cover is the least preferable way to use it unless you have no other option. Your attacker will be looking there and that is where they will expect you to appear. Whenever possible, shoot around the cover from the sides to mask your silhouette and make it more difficult for your enemy to see you.

Remember, we *Shoot Around Cover,* we do not rest our rifles on the cover. This is one aspect that is most often lost on people who engage in competitions and gun games where no one is down range shooting back.

Stay back from cover.

Move Your Feet

As often as not, the fight will begin because the bad guy has decided to initiate the attack. In this case, he knows where you are and has made a commitment to kill you. When you move, you are doing something that he/she did not anticipate and they will have to alter their plan, even slightly, in order to shoot you, stab you, or bust open your skull with a bat.

This is where we apply OODA and lessons taught by Colonel John Boyd. OODA stands for Observe, Orient, Decide, and Act. Every person engaged in combat goes through their own OODA, whether they are in a jet fighter or pointing a pistol at you.

John Boyd never lost a dogfight, and he participated in hundreds, because he understood OODA. The person who cycles through OODA the fastest is the person who will win the fight.

The simple act of moving your feet so that you are no longer in the place that your attacker expected you to be means that he has to restart his OODA. When you are ahead of him or inside his OODA, you have the tactical advantage.

A portion of Boyd's advice was that an important part of good tactics in a fight is to do what the enemy does not expect you to do. This actually goes all the way back to Sun Tzu and his Art of War. Miyamoto Musashi echoed this in the Book of Five Rings. When an attacker is given stimuli of which he has not expected or anticipated he is forced to begin his OODA loop from the beginning.

Understanding that we need to move our feet in a fight, it should now be obvious that we must train and practice shooting while we are moving. We do this on the training range to the point where it becomes natural and we will do it in the real world. If you are not shooting from around cover, you should be moving.

Situational Awareness

In order to move and shoot effectively, you must have your head up and be taking in all that is going on around you. Being situationally aware is a tactic that will not only help you defeat your attacker, but it will prevent you from negligently shooting the innocents or good guys who will very likely be around you.

Because it is important to keep your head up, we train and practice running our rifles without looking at them. A trained shooter should be able to load and load again, clear simple stoppages, disengage the safety, etc. without having to look at their rifle. If you are looking at your rifle, you are not looking at the world around you.

At first, new shooters might feel that they need to look at their guns to load them or clear stoppages. This is why we train. Also, if you are one of the people who feels a habitual need to look at your gun when you are working it, what will you do in darkness or poor light? If you cannot clear a stoppage without staring at your gun, how will you clear a stoppage when the light is poor or it is dark?

Somewhere in the neighborhood of 80 percent all sensory input comes from your vision in your normal, everyday life. During the stress, noise, and anxiety of a gunfight, nearly 100 percent of what you perceive will come from your vision. Staring at your rifle takes away your awareness of what is happening around you. If your vision is not focused on your sights, it should be focused on what is taking place around you.

Despite its age, the traditional carry handle AR-15 is still a formidable fighting tool.

Chapter 6

Optics and Accessories

Since 2004, the optic and accessory market for rifles has exploded. Two things were at play to make this happen. First, the terrorist attacks on 9/11/01 put us into a shooting war for the first time in two decades. Secondly, the Constitutionally unlawful "Crime Bill', which' did nothing to stop crime but everything to stifle lawful commerce, sunset and American gun buyers starting purchasing black rifles like no other time in the history of the nation. Both the US Government and the US consumer wanted stuff to add to their AR's and other rifles. This created a vast market for optics.

During this chapter we will primarily focus on the most useful and practical add-ons. However, when appropriate, warnings will be issued as well. Not every gadget for the AR, AK, etc. is valuable and some make the gun less reliable. That is a bad thing.

Engaging targets from a helicopter with EOTech equipped rifle.

Optics

When we are considering optical sights for our fighting rifle, we will focus on the 1:1 non-magnified variety. I know the Marine Corps bought thousands of 4x Trijicon ACOGs. Regardless, for the ranges that we will be engaging targets, a magnified optic is not necessary and in some cases will slow us down.

Since the 2004 Black Rifle Boom, optics for combat have come a long way and the improvements have been dramatic. The Top 3 contenders for US Military contracts have been: Aimpoint, Trijicon, and EOTech. Yes, EOTech had some trouble about ten years ago, but their Holographic Weapon Sight is a tremendous tool for rapid and accurate target acquisition. If you need to shoot things on the ground from a moving helicopter the EOTech HWS is the *GO TO* optic. Trust me on that. The downside of the HWS is battery-life compared to other comparable models.

For the layman, the EOTech HWS is a bit different of an animal than other red dots. The reticle of the HWS is actually a projected hologram. The "dot in circle" reticle that you see on the screen in front of your eye is a projected hologram and what this means from a practical standpoint is that after the sight has been zeroed it does not matter where you *perceive* the reticle to be on the screen, you can still hit your target as long as the red dot is on the target when you press the trigger. This is why the EOTech is so effective from the moving platform of a helicopter and when, due to circumstance, a less than ideal weapon mount is possible.

The EOTech is also the preferred optic for select-fire or suppressive fire weapons as the shooter simply focuses on keeping the target inside of the ring. The Marine Corps tried to put magnified ACOGs on machine guns and squad automatic weapons and that choice proved to be "less than optimum" to put it nicely. In other words, it was a shit show. The EOTech on a SAW (squad automatic weapon) or an M240 Bravo machine gun was a superior choice.

The EOTech uses a projected hologram.

Aimpoint optics have a rock solid reputation. For years the Comp M4 was the industry standard. The introduction of the Micro T1 and now the T2 set the standard for compact red dot optics. Are they free or cheap? No. With the Aimpoint you get what you pay for. In this case you get an optic that you can pass down to your grandkids.

The Trijicon ACOG and RMR are rhinoceros tough and can be had in Tritium or battery operated (for the RMR). I have used both. I do not have experience with the MRO model, but I have been told by people whose advice I trust that they are reliable.

Although it makes purists squirm, the Holosun brand of optics has proven to be extremely reliable. Communists can make good things if you hold their feet to the fire and watch them closely for quality assurance. Also, the idea that free men might be put in a position someday to make communists room temperature while using a Holosun brings a smile to my face.

Are their other companies making mini and micro red dot sights that work? Sure there are, the reality is that none of them yet have the track record for service that Aimpoint, Trijicon and EOTech have. Holosun is gaining a stellar reputation each day, month, and year.

If you are going to bet your life on a red dot optic you might want to spend more than a hundred dollars. Cheap optics are like cheap flashlights. They work until they don't and when they stop working is when you need them the most. It makes me want to vomit when I see people spend $1000 on a rifle and then stick an $89 optic on it. That just doesn't make sense.

When choosing an optic, be sure that it has the proper mounting system for your rifle. Some sights seem to be a bargain until you realize that it does not come with a mount that works with your rifle.

The Aimpoint Micro is compact and tough.

The Aimpoint P.R.O. is an excellent value.

Back Up Sights

If you choose not to purchase an optic and simply stick with the iron sights, then you don't need *back up sights.* However, when we are betting our lives on the performance of a rifle, redundancy is a good thing. Thanks to GWOT and the demand of the US Army for "same plane" optics, all of the quality, mil spec red dots will co-witness with standard height AR sights. *NOTE: Not all aftermarket sights for the AR are mil spec height. Let the buyer beware.

Back up sights come in two basic styles; straight up and canted. The straight up variety sit atop the rifle as you would expect and generally have the option to fold down. Canted sights are mounted on the rifle to the right and are 45° from up and down. Both work and canted sights can be exceedingly fast for close quarters fighting.

Battery life for modern optics has reached a nearly insane or unbelievable level. For example, the Trijicon MRO has a listed 5 year battery life. The Aimpoint T-2 Micro lists 50,000 hours of continuous run time. When it comes to back up sights, my main concern is not dead batteries, although that could technically happen.

Rain, snow, and mud can get onto the lens of an optic thus reducing its practical use. The canted back up sights are the perfect answer to that concern. Of course, it could be argued that snow and mud could get on the iron sights too. Hell, the world is an imperfect place.

Slings

As we discussed in the shotgun book, the two primary types of slings for fighting long guns are the single point and traditional double or two point or parade slings. Both have their fans and detractors. A single point sling is a good choice for those who carry a sidearm as a backup should their rifle stop working unexpectedly. For general field carry, the single point sling is less beneficial. However, it is far better to have a single point sling than it is to be setting your rifle down constantly so you can use both hands.

For the standard, two-point sling the rifle can be carried in an administrative fashion over the dominant or support shoulder. Also, a standard sling can be looped over the neck and used as you would a single point. In this fashion, if both hands are needed, the shooter simply lets go of the rifle and it hangs on the front of the body. Transitioning to a sidearm can be done when the rifle is carried in such a way.

Aftermarket Triggers

One of the items that American shooters have been convinced that they *must have* is an aftermarket trigger for their fighting rifle. Light, match-tuned triggers or polished triggers add to enhanced accuracy in precision guns that we will shoot slowly and deliberately, that is not the purpose of the ballistic sledgehammer.

The primary issue with aftermarket triggers is that they can be so light that they fail to ignite the primers on military ammunition or even some commercial ammunition. If you get a light primer strike during a shooting match, it's not the end of the world. If you are in a fight for your life and the hammer is not making the cartridges go "boom", you could die for your choice.

The stock triggers on AR and AK fighting guns might seem *heavy* but trust me, that is perception. In the Corps, we shot human-sized silhouette targets at 500 yards using iron sights and stock Mil Spec triggers. Before you decide that you absolutely must have a new trigger for your fighting gun, take a 2 day class and put 300-400 rounds through your gun. If you still want a new trigger after the class is over, go for it.

Oversized / Ambi Controls

This is the warning part of the chapter. The controls on a gun that was built and designed for fighting were made that way based upon rigorous field testing. There is a big difference between shooting your rifle from the comfort of a shooting bench at your favorite range and carrying a rifle out in the real world.

Aftermarket controls tend to stick out and catch on clothing, gear, and even gloved hands. They also can be less than robust or fragile when used in field conditions. Oversized magazine release buttons are a great way to accidentally drop your magazine in the field. Oversized charging handles love to catch and hang up on load-bearing gear and clothing. Just as we discussed with the trigger issue, before you decide you must alter your gun with aftermarket controls, take the stock rifle to a training course and run it for two full days in realistic conditions.

Gloves

Though technically not a *firearm accessory*, shooting gloves are a valuable *range/field accessory*. If you are going to run a stock AK, you absolutely should be wearing gloves. If you choose to run your AK in training minus gloves, you will experience "Mikhail's Revenge". The AK will cut you in places you never imagined and the handguards and barrel are going to get HOT. This applies for all fighting rifles.

Gloves are worn in the field to protect your hands. Other than your vision, your hands are the most important things you will need to run the gun. If your hands are bleeding or burned, your ability to run the gun will be diminished to say the least. Also, people who say you cannot shoot a rifle accurately with gloves on are full of shit. I wore gloves during a sniper training school and fired every single round with a full glove on my shooting hand. No, I did not cut off the trigger finger. That, kids, is pure fucktardation.

Many companies sell quality shooting gloves that both protect your hands and allow you to employ your guns. Thanks again to GWOT, more brands of gloves are available than ever before. You can walk into any auto parts store in America and try on Mechanix gloves for size. Find the size that fits you just right and purchase two pairs of identical gloves. You will thank me later.

Fighting Lights

Just as we discussed during the book on martial application of the pistol, we cannot morally or legally shoot as scary sounds or dark shadows. You are responsible for every single round you fire. If your bullet strikes someone or something that it should not have, you own it. We cannot simply apologize and move on.

Mounting a powerful, white light onto a fighting rifle is a valuable and morally responsible action. Surefire is the top of the game in this regard as they have the longest and best track record. Streamlight comes a close second to Surefire and their products have proven to be reliable.

Keep in mind that not all lights are "impact resistant". The recoil of your rifle is going to put strain on not only the lamp of your light, but the internal components. Discount store lights are not built to withstand the pounding of being mounted to the front of a rifle. Just as we discussed with optics, a cheap light is going to work until it does not and it will break when you need it the most.

When you mount a light on your rifle it should be secured with quality aluminum mounting hardware and you need to put thread-lock on the screws. *Note: put thread-lock on ALL of the screws on your rifle.

Surefire weapon light on AR.

Visible and IR Lasers and Night Vision

Although this might seem monotonous, the advancement in visible and infrared laser target designators and night vision gear has surpassed that which many of us thought possible twenty years ago. Again, we can thank the US Government / US Army demand for these items.

The use of such items is a bit more advanced than we have the time or inclination to discuss at length here in this book. As you advance in your skill level, you may decide to invest in such items. Understand that night vision and laser designators will cost as much as you paid for the rifle and optics, perhaps a bit more.

The one piece of advice I would offer here is that if you anticipate that one day you will want to add a night vision monocular to your rifle, when you purchase a red dot optic, get one that is "Night Vision Compatible", not all of them are. You will know this because the illumination setting on the optic is marked "NV".

Muzzle Devices

Twenty or even fifteen years ago, the idea that the end user would deliberately remove and switch out the muzzle device that came on their rifle from the factory was almost unheard of. The majority of gun buyers took it in good faith that the manufacturer had put the best muzzle device on the barrel. The aftermarket muzzle device catalog was thin and limited to specialists and custom gun makers. As I write these words, that is no longer the case.

American gun buyers are more familiar with the mechanical working of their guns than ever before, thanks in large part to online videos. Also, the rise of the shooting Instagram model has caused many gun owners to believe that they need to alter their rifle to be more like the one used by their favorite "influencer" (puke).

Muzzle Devices come in various configurations.

Flash Hiders, Compensators, and Muzzle Brakes

Rifles are loud and in reduced light conditions they can create a huge flash or fireball. Long ago, the military realized that giving away your position to the enemy by creating a large orange fireball while simultaneously flash-blinding your troops was a poor choice, if given the option not to do so.

Firearms manufacturers began to address both the noise and flash situation by creating muzzle devices designed to tame the beast. We should all understand that it is the expanding propellant gas that creates both the noise and flash.

Let's consider the Flash Hider first. One of the oldest examples of a flash hider was the device mounted to the M1 "Jungle Carbine". It was the addition of the conical shaped flash hider that distinguished the Jungle Carbine from the standard M1 Carbine. The 3-prong, split flash hider on the original XM16A1 was actually very effective at controlling the flash of the 5.56mm cartridge. The "Vortex" flash hider is one of the best, modern examples of this design.

The current M16A2/M4 muzzle device acts as a hybrid flash hider / compensator. The A2 flash hider is open on top and closed on the bottom. This helps to reduce visible flash and the rise of the muzzle as well as reducing a dust signature when the shooter is firing from the prone.

A Compensator muzzle device on a rifle is primarily there to reduce muzzle rise and help the shooter control the gun during rapid or automatic fire. The compensator has been around quite a long time and can be found in various configurations from simple to complex. The famous AK "Slant Brake" is actually not a muzzle brake at all, it is a compensator that was designed to aid the shooter in controlling the muzzle rise from the 7.62x39mm cartridge.

The Muzzle Brake is similar to the compensator as it is made to address and control the escaping propellant gas. However, the modern incarnation of the muzzle brake on rifles has become a device that directs the gas from the cartridge to the sides and slightly rearward. Muzzle brakes are not designed to hide the flash from the gas and many function as "flash enhancers" not hiders.

The muzzle brake does indeed reduce the felt recoil of the rifle. On a firearm, such as the Barrett M82A1, you would definitely not want to shoot the gun without one. The idea that the recoil from the 5.56mm or even 7.62x39mm is so severe that it must be controlled by a brake is a bit ludicrous.

Also, the modern muzzle brake has become known as the *competition brake* because of its use by shooting match competitors. The muzzle brake or comp brake serves to both direct the noise from the shot back toward the shooter and anyone with the misfortune to be near them as well and blast gas into the face of that same person. Competition brakes or muzzle brakes have NO BUSINESS on a rifle that is designated for fighting or martial application.

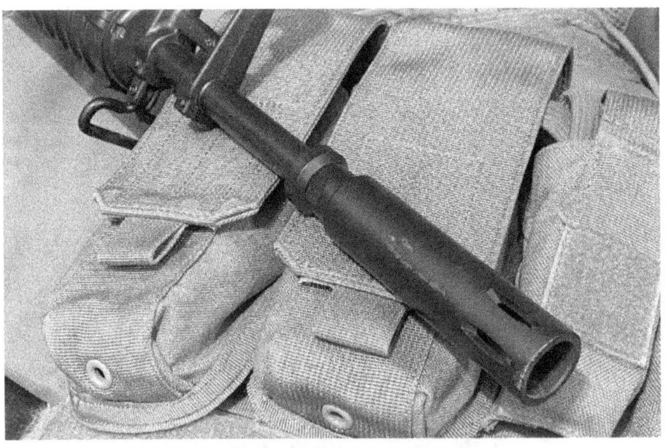

The XM177E2 flash hider

There are numerous effective and useful muzzle devices for the modern rifle. The XM177E2 flash hider or "moderator" is a fantastic example. The moderator not only controls the flash from the 5.56mm cartridge, but it effectively pushes or directs the expanding gas away from the shooter's face and anyone who might be fighting alongside the shooter. The only downside to the XM177 device is that it adds length to the gun.

Spike's Tactical offers a device that both controls flash and directs the gas away from the shooter while controlling muzzle rise. Spike's calls this device "The Barking Spider". The Barking Spider uses a chamber/baffle system to trap and dampen the expanding gas. While a bit pricey, this is an excellent muzzle device for reducing muzzle climb, flash, and pushing the noise away from the shooter's face.

Speaking of noise, the closer the muzzle is to the shooter's face, the more important the muzzle device becomes. With the rise in popularity of the rifle caliber pistol with short and super short barrels, pushing the noise away from the shooter and controlling the flash are important considerations.

The Barking Spider from Spikes Tactical

Silencers, Suppressors, Moderators

Whether you call them silencers, suppressors, sound moderators, gun mufflers, cans, whatever, these devices act to quiet the noise, reduce the flash and dust signature, and control the muzzle rise.

For those of you who like to argue over semantics, let's consider historical facts. It was related to me at least a dozen years ago, by an expert in the gun muffler field, that the original patent application filed in 1908 by Hiram Percy Maxim (son of the machine gun designer) was for the "Silent Firearm". His company was the Maxim Silent Firearms Co. So, if you want to argue that the term "silencer" is incorrect, you would be taking on the man who invented the thing.

As mentioned previously, the firearms silencer performs the job of a flash hider, a compensator, a muzzle brake, and acts as an effective gun muffler. No, a suppressor on a rifle does not make the gun shot *silent.* However, the ear splitting noise of a 5.56, 7.62x39, etc. is dampened to levels we can call *hearing safe* when a can is installed.

Despite the government red tape and hassle, purchasing and using a firearm silencer is well worth the effort. Yes, it takes time to complete the process. Keep in mind that time is always going to pass. If you start now, time will pass and you will end up with an extremely useful firearms accessory that you will be glad to have once you begin using it.

Chapter 7   BZO and Sighting

BZO is a military acronym for "Battle Sight Zero". We BZO our iron sights or our optic at a distance that fits with the range we will practically be engaging targets. For the fighting rifle, there has been some contention in the popular press as to what distance this is.

When I was in the Marine Corps infantry, we would BZO the iron sights on our M-16A2 at 25 meters. If you make the command decision to BZO at 30 yards or 50 meters or even 100m, that is up to you. The primary point of the exercise is to know exactly where your sights are set and to make adjustments accordingly. Remember, bullets do not fly straight like laser beams, they rise and fall.

With a red dot optic, BZO is as simple as adjusting the elevation and windage setting on the optic. Take the time to refer to your owner's manual for the specific optic for adjustments. Not every optic is the same. Some have ¼ MOA adjustments, some are ½ MOA and some are ⅓ MOA.

Read the manual, knob adjustments vary from maker to maker and optic to optic.

When your sights or optic are BZO'd, you should be able to put rounds reliably on human sized targets from ranges as close as 5 yards out to even 300 yards. Yes, 300 yards is a long shot for a self-defense rifle; 5 to 50 yards is generally the sweet spot with which we are primarily concerned.

What kind of accuracy can you expect? When firing slowly from a supported position, the three-shot triangle you fire should be in the neighborhood of one inch across. Yes, even the AK will put rounds into a 1 inch group at that distance. The 5.56mm AR will likely group them tighter if the shooter does their job.

While we are discussing sighting, you need to be aware of this thing we call "Mechanical Offset". Mechanical offset is the physical distance between the bore of the barrel and the aiming device; be it front sight or reticle. Normal offset is going to be around 2.5 to 3 inches. The original AK has a mechanical offset of 45mm or 1.7 inches. What that means is that the bullet path is actually 1.7, 2.5 or 3 inches below where your eye perceives the sights to be. The closer you are to the target the more important this is.

I would venture to say that we have all seen at least one video online where the shooter puts rounds into their truck hood or roof because they neglected to compensate for offset. This is another reason why we shoot *around* cover and do not hug up against it. There have been real world instances where shooters shot into the cover they were using even though their sights were on the target. If you fire a 5.56 or 7.62 bullet into a brick wall two feet in front of you, it's going to get your attention.

Why 25 Meters?

You may be justifiably wondering why did the US Military choose 25 meters as their BZO distance? We know that bullets do not fly straight, like lasers, but they rise and fall after leaving the muzzle. Given the ballistics of the 5.56mm round, with the sights set at 25 meters, if the shooter holds on target with a center chest or sternum sight picture, they will be able to hit a man-sized target from 25 meters to 300 meters without making any sight adjustments. They are not going to hit him in the sternum at every distance between 25 and 300, but the bullets will hit the enemy if the shooter does their job.

Even when rifles have adjustable rear sights, military commanders do not expect soldiers to make contact with the enemy, estimate the distance, adjust their sights appropriately, and then engage. That is the job of snipers, not infantry soldiers. The 25 meter BZO ensures that the windage and elevation are correct and gives a "happy medium" or a practical compromise for engaging the enemy at varied distances.

The Front Sight Post

I have encountered numerous gun owners who have purchased a rifle with adjustable iron sights, disregarded the "Owner's Manual", and tried to zero their gun by using the adjustable rear sight only.

Whether we are discussing the AR, the AK, the FAL, etc., if the rifle in question has an adjustable rear sight, chances are good that it has a front sight that is adjustable for elevation and sometimes windage (AK).

When setting a BZO with a rifle that has both an adjustable front and rear sight, you need to begin by ensuring that the rear sight is bottomed out or set at the lowest setting. Bench the rifle onto/into a solid, stable rest and slow-fire 3 shots. Take your time.

Examine what should be a nice, tight triangle of shot holes. Make your adjustments based upon what would be the center of the triangle. All BZO adjustments for elevation are made using the front sight post, NOT the rear sight.

The current Mil Spec standard for the M-16/M4 front sight post is quarter increment adjustments either up or down. For the M4, one "click" of adjustment moves the strike of the round approximately ½ inch at 25 meters. At 100 meters, the same click equals a 1 ⅞ inch adjustment. *See US Army M4/M16 User's Manual, TM 9-1005-319-10.

For the standard AK rifle, the front sight post is NOT click adjustable and it is more of a typical threading. One full 360° revolution of the front sight adjusts the bullet impact up or down by 20 centimeters at 100 meters. What this translates to is 5 centimeters per quarter turn at 100m. A quarter turn of the front sight will move the impact 1.25cm at 25m.

Most M4 front sights will be tight when they are fresh out of the box. Flip the rifle upside down and you will see a lubrication port under the A-frame front sight housing. Put one or two drops of oil in that hole before making sight adjustments. The M-16 sights were designed by Gene Stoner to be adjusted by using the tip of a full metal jacket 5.56mm bullet. There are also special tools for adjusting AR front sights. Windage adjustments for the M4 or AR are made with the rear sight.

For the AK you will need a specially designed tool to adjust the front sight up and down. (Like the M4, you can turn the AK upside down and drip some lubrication onto the threads of the front sight post.) This AK sight tool is also used to push the front sight left or right to adjust for windage. You could pound on the front sight with a mallet, but trust me, if you own an AK, or two, buy the AK sight tool.

Keep in mind, when adjusting a front sight, we move the post in the opposite direction that we want the impact of the bullet to move. If you want the strike of the round to move up, we lower the front sight and vice versa. For the AK, if you need the bullet impact to move to the right, you push the front sight post to the left. The rear sight on a rifle is a true adjustment, left for left, right for right, up for up, and down for down.

With the front sight of your rifle now properly BZO'd, all adjustments for elevation using the rear sight will be as true as possible as long as you are using the ammunition for which the gun was built.

If you own an AK, invest in an AK front sight tool.

Chapter 8 Ammunition Selection and Mags

As with any type of firearm, we need to consider the ammunition we decide to use, as well as for what purpose. The rifle is no different in this regard than the pistol or the shotgun. When we consider the rifle as a fighting tool there may be some confusion as to which ammunition to select for which mission.

The two basic criteria or areas to consider are; training and personal defense. Can both be interchangeable? Yes, to a certain extent, they can be. For instance, the US Military uses the M193, the M885, the SS109 and Mk262 5.56mm for both training and combat. All of the aforementioned loads are Mil Spec or meet the military specifications for issue.

Of course, the United States Government buys ammunition with OPM (other people's money). If you are using your own money to purchase training ammunition, you are going to want to purchase the best ammo for the best price.

Every major ammunition maker in the United States produces both a training ammunition line and a premium defensive line for rifles. Federal Cartridge has the American Eagle line, Remington has UMC, and Winchester has their ubiquitous USA or "White Box" ammunition. Full metal jacket from PMC Ammunition, if you can find it, is great for training.

Due to the great ammo crisis of the 2020's, numerous foreign imports have begun to pop up online and on store shelves. Most of it is pretty good, having been made in the same factories overseas that produce ammunition for that country's military.

Just as we discussed in the pistol book, manufacturers put higher quality components into ammunition that is designated for fighting/combat than they do for practice/training ammo. Again, the projectiles, cases, propellent powder, and primers in Mil Spec or defensive ammunition go through rigorous QA inspection. Military ammunition will also be produced with a flash-reducing powder in most cases, where practice ammunition will not.

Bullets

Do the bullets or projectiles in fighting ammunition absolutely have to be a controlled-expansion design? That is a valid question. The honest answer is; no, they do not absolutely have to be controlled-expansion in order for the rifle to be a valid fighting tool. However, from a scientific or ballistic standpoint, the smaller the caliber, the more important the bullet design will be. The .223 Winchester or 5.56mm NATO tremendously benefits from use of the BTHP or OTM bullets. The Mk262 uses a 77 grain OTM bullet and that round has proven in combat to be a tremendous man-stopper.

Nonetheless, a 55 grain full metal jacket bullet traveling around 3000 feet per second is nothing to sneeze at. The shooter simply needs to understand that multiple rounds may need to be fired AND full metal jacket projectiles are far more likely to enter and exit the target animal than would an OTM or BTHP style bullet.

Steel-Cased Ammunition

Some folks love steel-cased ammo and some folks hate it. The reality is that steel-cased ammunition came into being because it was less expensive to manufacture than standard brass cased ammunition. The Soviet Union needed/wanted millions upon millions of rounds of 7.62x39mm ammo and they were able to make it more economically than they could have with brass.

Over the decades numerous companies have offered steel-cased ammunition as an economical option for American shooters. Generally, steel-cased ammo runs just fine in pistols and it runs great in the guns for which it was originally made: Soviet/Russian designs. Firearms chambered in 7.62x39mm, 5.45x39mm, 7.62x54R all feed and cycle steel-cased ammunition perfectly well.

Now we come to the .223 and .308, both very popular American calibers. In the USA, the AR-15 was built and designed to feed a brass-cased cartridge. Will AR's feed and cycle steel-cased ammo? Yes and no. Most of them will feed and cycle steel-cased ammunition up to the point where the chamber gets superheated. This is when the wheels tend to come off. Stuck casings and stuck cartridges when using steel-cased ammunition occur not after a few shots, but after strings of fire. Such stuck cases will NOT just fall out but must be knocked out using a stiff range rod / cleaning rod.

Black Hills Ammunition makes the highest quality fighting ammo for rifles and pistols.

The advice of most firearm training experts is this, use steel-cased ammunition for the guns it was made for; Commies guns. For American made guns, use brass-cased ammunition. If you follow that advice you will not likely go wrong. If you still want to shoot steel-cased ammo in an AR, remember to take a cleaning rod to the range.

Magazines

While we are on the topic of ammunition, we should also discuss the devices used to feed that ammunition into our martial rifle. One piece of good news is that more magazines have been manufactured for the Stoner-based AR in the last ten years than during the previous fifty. The less than good news is that the quality of these magazines has varied from good to great to poor in some cases.

Mil Spec aluminum magazines produced to meet government contract requirements are reliable and relatively inexpensive. In 2018, the United States Marine Corps, after years of testing, officially adopted the Magpul PMAG as the official issue for its men. The Gen M3 PMAG is the current standard. Gen 2 PMAGs are plentiful on the market and will work. The Gen M3 magazines are just a bit better.

One of the primary reasons we are discussing magazines is due to the fact that most rifle manufacturers ship their guns with one, single magazine. The minimum requirement for a fighting rifle is six (6) quality magazines. There are numerous off-brand, aftermarket magazines out there. The magazines on which you can bet your life are the aluminum Mil Spec versions and the Magpul PMAGS. Saving one or two dollars on a discount magazine is not worth the hassle or the potential life-threatening failure.

Also, just as we do with pistol magazines, take a paint pen and mark your magazines with numbers. If you begin to experience stoppages, take note of the magazine number. Multiple failures with magazine #4, or whichever, means it needs to go in the garbage and be replaced.

How many rounds should I load in a 30 round magazine?

The US Military has been the prime culprit for perpetuating the "downloading" of magazines mythology. Back in the Old Corp, we were required, when carrying our M1911A1 pistols on duty, to have only 5 rounds loaded into the seven round magazines. During the same time, we were taught to only load 28 rounds into 30 rounds M-16 magazines.

A suspicion that I had while I was on active duty was confirmed to me when I was working as a Military Contractor for a Training Command. The military refuses to throw away worn out magazines or even replace the springs in them. The US Military will allot money for the most retarded shit imaginable, but they will not allot the money to replace magazines on a regular basis.

The reason why we were told to only load 5 rounds into 7 rounds M1911A1 magazines is because, by the late 1980's, most of the magazines were over 40 years old having been produced for WWII. I had an armorer explain to me that loading 28 rounds into 30 round M-16 magazines "saves the springs". I'm sure that man did not come up with that on his own, but that is what he had been told.

When I went to work for a Training Command in 2007 during GWOT, we stood up that particular school. That is, we started from scratch. We were the first instructors with the very first students. The supply personnel for the school ordered "X" number of brand new, aluminum GI mags for our M4's. Three years and thousands of students later, they had purchased a total of zero (0) replacement magazines. When students began having frequent stoppages, particularly Type 3 double-feeds with their M4's, the instructor corp began to look closely at the magazines. Many of them had feed lips that were out of spec.

When we addressed the magazine problems and suggested removing the magazines from inventory, we were told "Just teach them how to clear stoppages, that's your job." The problem was that students were beginning to lose faith in the guns that they were supposed to be carrying in combat to save their lives.

The solution that we came up with as the instrurctor corps was to identify the out of spec magazines, take them behind the ammo tent and crush those fuckers with a blunt instrumment. We'd throw them back in the empty ammo crate used for magazine storage and the problem began to sort itself out.

As an armed citizen, it is up to you to know when to trash a used-up/out of spec magazine. Your life is too valuable to trust to an "iffy" mag. Spend the $15 or $20 and move on.

One of the issues with older aluminum M-16 magazines was the inability to lock the magazine in place on a closed bolt. In order to get a magazine to seat and lock under a closed bolt (or slide) the rounds in the magazine need to give or be depressed a fraction of an inch. If the follower is bottomed out and the rounds in the magazine will not depress, even a fraction of an inch, the magazine will not lock securely in place. The Army's and the Marine Corp's solution for this is to have troopers download by two rounds. A fully loaded 30 round magazine will seat in a rifle with an open bolt without issue. Of course, the AK does not have such a problem so there is no need to download AK mags.

All of the 7.62mm NATO battle rifles that I have used have no problems seating a full 20 round magazine on a closed bolt. The author would suggest that you try seating a fully loaded magazine on the closed bolt of your personal rifle and see how it works. It is always best to operate based upon experience versus gun shop or shooting range gossip or hearsay.

The GI MilSpec Aluminum and the Magpul Gen3 PMags are the most reliable AR/M4 magazines.

Operator running an M-16 style rifle.

Bonus Chapter

Black Rifle Build Project

One of the greatest benefits to myself, the author of this and the other Martial Application books, is that the production of these texts has given me the opportunity to examine the topics in great detail.

Colonel Jeff Cooper, USMC, the founder of Gunsite Training Academy and the father of modern pistolcraft, decades ago closely examined the M1911A1 pistol. At the time, the M1911A1 was the standard for fighting pistols in the world. However, the .45 acp service pistol was not perfect.

Col. Cooper instructed the Gunsite armorer to make certain modifications to the stock M1911A1 before it could be called a "Gunsite Pistol". The resulting handgun was described by Jeff as having "everything you need and nothing that you don't."

Yes, I do remember that this is a rifle book. While examining the modern AR-15 style rifle, I thought about Col. Cooper's mission to produce a minimalist fighting gun that had what you needed without adding things that you did not. I suppose you could call this a ballistic MED (minimum effective dose) project.

Sadly, the state of our industry has people purchasing and adding things to rifles that are often highly suspect and do little more than clutter the gun and make it heavier. Yes, that lead-up is my way of saying that I decided to build an AR-15 style rifle with the idea that I would come up with a minimalist, no clutter/no fluff gun.

One of the first places I went to was the Brownells website to start browsing and get ideas.

Lower Receiver

About 15 or 16 years ago I borrowed an AR-style rifle from James Yeager to participate in a Fighting Rifle class. The gun was unique as it was built on CAV Arms polymer, unibody lower receiver. The concept of a unibody AR lower receiver was revived by Brownells in partnership with KE Arms.

The KE Arms complete AR lower is unique in that it combines the stock, pistol grip and receiver into one unit. This makes the gun lightweight and relatively inexpensive to manufacture. The savings naturally are passed on to the consumer.

The stock on the lower is fixed, which is perfectly acceptable. Stock length is A1 not A2, meaning it has a 13 inch LOP (Length of Pull). True M16A1 stock LOP is 12.875" and the A2 is 13.5 inches.

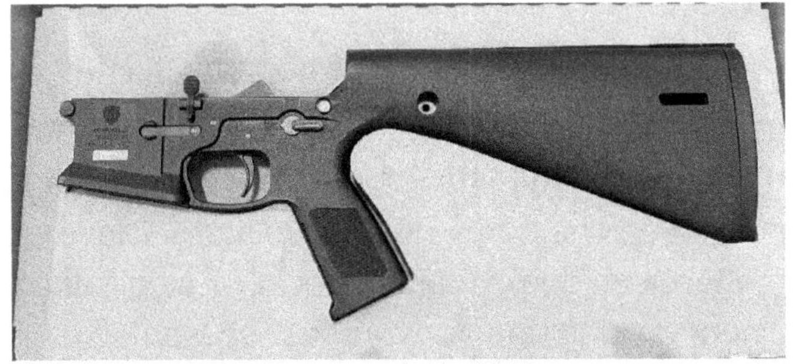

KE Arms unibody lower

Upper Receiver

For the upper receiver, I looked in my shop and into a bin of AR parts that I have been accumulating for decades. A good while back, my friend Randy Luth, founder of DPMS and Luth AR, sent me a box of AR parts. One of the parts was a stripped AR upper receiver that was unique in that it had no forward assist (FA) mechanism nor a spring-loaded dust cover. However, the upper did include M1913 Picatinny rails, not just on the top, but on the left and right.

I must confess, I used all of the other AR parts that Randy sent me, but that upper receiver has been sitting in my parts bin waiting for me to do something with it. Well, the time is now. (This is one reason I never get rid of miscellaneous gun parts.)

You might be thinking, "But, there is no forward assist, the gun won't work." Folks, I have been running an M16/M4/AR for better than 30 years now. Searching my memory, and I have a pretty clear one, I cannot recall a single time when tapping the forward assist was what I needed to do to keep the gun running. Yes, a dirty, dusty, gritty AR bolt might need a push on the rarest occasion. That is why Gene Stoner put the bevel or cut out on the bolt carrier, so you could nudge it with your thumb or finger.

What I have witnessed throughout the years is that tapping the forward assist on the M4/AR has become a nervous tick for shooters. I've seen them load their rifle and then take their dominant hand off of the grip to tap the FA. Generally they tap it at least twice.

There is very little wiggle room in the chamber of a rifle. If the bolt refuses to seat after you have nudged the BCG with your thumb, something is awry. Fun story. Back when I was training the military, we were on a field exercise where the troops were firing blanks from their M4's. One young man had loaded his blank 5.56mm cartridges in his magazine backwards. Yes, that happened.

When this young trooper attempted to chamber a round, the backward blank cartridge naturally failed to chamber and the bolt was half open. Undaunted, the man pounded away on the forward assist mechanism until the cartridge was driven into the chamber, hard. We had quite a fun time driving the blank cartridge out of the chamber. The young man, in his defense, had been taught that if the bolt failed to seat, he was to push the FA until it did so. No one had ever said to this young man, "If the bolt does not close with one tap, STOP!"

**DPMS upper, now unobtanium, but Luth AR
has a similar part.**

Barrel

As this build will be for a rifle not a rifle caliber pistol, I need an AFT friendly length. I returned to the Brownells website and selected a Brownells brand 16-inch carbine length barrel with an A2 front sight housing. The barrel came with all of the mounting hardware, save a gas tube. A gas tube of the corresponding length was ordered as well.

The barrel ships minus a muzzle device, for this I decided to go with a low profile Yankee Hill Manufacturing flash hider. This part and the

Magpul BUIS rear back-up sight also were picked up from Brownells.

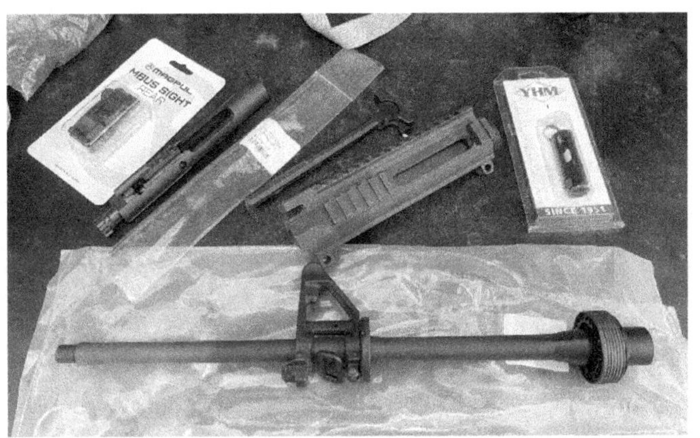

Barrel and some parts ordered from Brownells catalog.

Other Parts

Diving back into my parts bin, I had a complete AR-15 bolt carrier group and I must admit that I have more AR charging handles than I have rifles. The KE Arms complete lower receiver would arrive with the trigger, buffer and spring and all the various controls and parts necessary.

I have assembled numerous AR lowers in my time. For this project I did not feel like I needed the practice. Besides, for the price, I was perfectly happy to let KE Arms install the trigger, bolt hold-open, magazine catch, etc.

Regarding the handguard or the forend, I decided to order an MOE version from Magpul as well as a cantilever rail mount to pair with the handguard. One accessory that any defensive rifle must have is a white light. I would be adding one to the gun for this project. The last item I ordered from Magpul was black Gen3 Pmags.

Assembly

The KE Arms lower, being the "firearm" portion, had to be picked up from our FFL guy. The rest of the parts arrived in brown boxes from Brownells and Magpul. Laying all of the parts out on my workbench, I visualized the assembly process. That is when I realized that the gas tube did not come with the tiny little roll pin needed to secure it in place in the front sight housing.

Fortunately, I have been at this game for quite a long time. Back to my parts tote I went. Inside the bin was a ziplock bag full of miscellaneous AR parts; detent pins, tiny springs, clips, gas rings and, yes, a teenie, tiny roll pin for the gas tube.

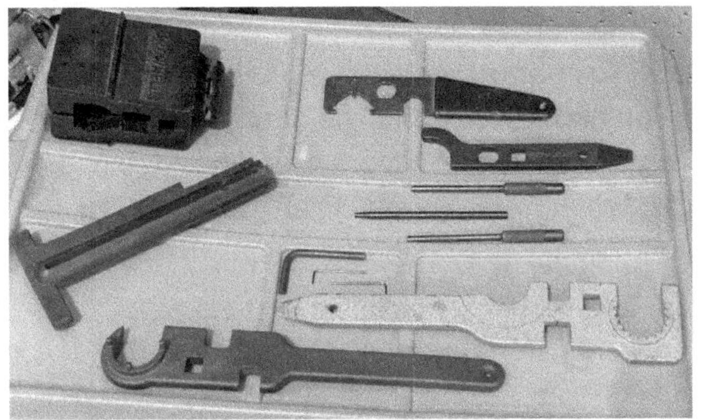

A variety of AR builder tools from Brownells catalog.

A piece of advice, if you have never assembled an AR before, skip Youtube and go straight to the Brownells website and watch their "How to Build an AR-15" series. Back in the old days, I watched the DVD version. Not only will their professional gunsmiths show you how to put it all together, they will recommend the dedicated tools to get the job done right. At the very least, you are going to need an M4/AR Armorer's wrench and a roll pin punch set.

Also, remember to get some threadlock compound. All the threads on your AR should be coated with threadlock before final assembly.

With the upper receiver fully assembled, it was time to mate it with the KE Arms lower. The pivot and takedown pins that come with the unibody lower are more like an HK pin than traditional AR pins. They can be pulled completely out and then re-installed.

A.R.M.E.D. rifle assembled with parts from Brownells and Magpul.

Take note; even though the pivot and takedown pins look similar, they are different lengths, just like a typical AR. It is possible to inadvertently switch them which this author might have done. Swapping these pins will allow an ever so slight play between the upper and lower receivers which can and will cause stoppages.

At press time, we have only put about 100 rounds through the A.R.M.E.D. As long as the author ensured the takedown and pivot pins were in the correct holes, the gun ran fine. We will be testing it much more, but production deadlines need to be met and books need to be printed.

For Training; you are encouraged to go to www.SOTGU.com for more information.

Additional Books from the Author

Student of the Gun Instructor Development Manual

Precision Rifle Range Book

Martial Application of the Pistol

Martial Application of the Shotgun

Patriot Fire Team Manual

Patriot Fire Team Equipment Guide

Patriot Fire Team Mission Planner

Mr. Markel's professional education includes:

- Executive Security International
    - Executive Protection and Bodyguard studies
    - Intelligence Gathering and Investigation
    - Advanced Firearms training under John S. Farnam

- **United States Marine Corps** service training *Combat Decorated Veteran*
    - Basic Training: Physical Fitness, Rifle Marksmanship, Swim Qualification, First Aid, Marine Corps History and Traditions
    - School of the Infantry: Anti-Tank Assault, Patrolling, Ambush Techniques, Nighttime and Low Light Operations
    - Sea Service Indoctrination School: Shipboard Firefighting and Damage Control, Naval Service traditions, Advanced Physical Training, Advanced Marksmanship Training, Customs and Courtesies
    - Shipboard Security Engagement Training (SSET) and Nuclear Weapons Storage and Security School, Fast Reaction Team training

- - Demolitions, Mines and Explosive Ordnance School
  - USMC Marksmanship Coaches School
  - Desert Survival Training
  - Jungle Warfare Indoctrination and Patrolling
  - USMC Leadership Training / NCO Course

- Ohio State Peace Officers Academy (State Police Academy)

- Special Weapons and Tactics Manual Structure Breaching School

- Advanced Firearms Training Courses
  - Gunsite Academy: Rifle, Pistol, Shotgun courses
  - Tactical Defense Institute: Close Quarters Fighting, Pistol, and Rifle courses
  - SIG Academy: Pistol, Carbine, Shotgun, Long Range Rifle courses
  - Tactical Response: Fighting Pistol and Fighting Rifle, Close Quarters Fighting courses, Fight Strong Strength Training

- - Ken Hackathorn: Advanced Handgun and Carbine Course
  - International Tactical Training Systems: Urban Sniper School
  - Blackwater Academy: Advanced Shotgun course
  - Expeditionary Combat Skills: Advanced Rifle and Pistol, Tactical Combat Casualty Care, Judgment-based Engagement Training

- Instructor Courses
  - SureFire Academy: Low Light Tactics Instructor School
  - U.S.M.C. Marksmanship Coaches School
  - U.S. Navy Marksmanship Coaches School
  - Tidewater Community College Instructor Training Course
  - Oleoresin Capsicum Aerosol Training Instructor Trainer School
  - Red Cross CPR and Family First Aid Instructor course
  - National Rifle Association: Handgun, Rifle, and Shotgun Instructor School, Range Safety Officers School,

- NRA Law Enforcement Handgun and Shotgun Instructor school
- National 4H Youth Firearms Instructors School

Mr. Markel has been teaching safe and effective firearms handling to students young and old for decades and has worked actively with the 4-H Shooting Sports program. Paul holds numerous instructor certifications in multiple disciplines; nonetheless, he is and will remain a dedicated Student of the Gun